Walk 2

GLENFINNAN

Distance
3 miles / 4.75 km

Time
1¾ hours

GO BY TRAIN · CATCH A BUS

Start/Finish
Glenfinnan

Parking PH37 4LT
Glenfinnan Community
car park

Cafés/pubs
Visitor centre;
Glenfinnan Station

Sensational
views over Loch
Shiel, Glenfinnan
Viaduct and
Monument

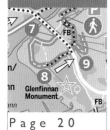

Page 20

W...

S...
B...

GW00750267

Distance
3.25 miles / 5.2 km

Time
1¾ hours

GO BY TRAIN · CATCH A BUS

Start/Finish
Commando Memorial

Parking PH34 4EG
Commando Memorial
car park

Cafés/pubs
Nearest in Spean
Bridge

Magnificent
viewpoint; historic
bridge; railway
path; Grey Corries
scene

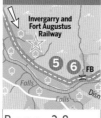

Page 28

Distance
3.2 miles / 5.1 km

Time
1¾ hours

GO BY TRAIN · CATCH A BUS

Start/Finish
Banavie

Parking PH33 7PL
Neptune's Staircase
car park

Cafés/pubs
The Moorings Hotel;
An Cafaidh Mara

Picnic beside the
canal; wonderful
staircase locks;
Ben Nevis views

Page 34

Walk 5	Walk 6	Walk 7

Walk 5

FORT WILLIAM

Distance
3.2 miles/5.1km

Time
1¾ hours

Start/Finish
An-Aird, Fort William

Parking PH33 6EW
An-Aird No. 1 car park

Cafés/pubs
Larder Café; Fort William

Ruined fort; medieval castle; Great Glen Way; Loch Linnhe; River Lochy

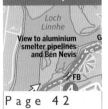

Page 42

Walk 6

GLEN NEVIS

Distance
2.75 miles/4.4km

Time
1½ hours

Start/Finish
Ben Nevis Visitor Centre

Parking PH33 6ST
Glen Nevis Visitor Centre car park

Cafés/pubs
Snacks at visitor centre; Glen Nevis Restaurant/Bar

Majestic Glen Nevis and Ben Nevis views; the West Highland Way

Page 48

Walk 7

KINLOCHLEVEN

Distance
2.6 miles/4.1km

Time
1½ hours

Start/Finish
Kinlochleven

Parking PH50 4RU
Kinlochleven public car park

Cafés/pubs
Kinlochleven

Riverside walk; stunning view down Loch Leven; hydropower; Aluminium Story

Page 54

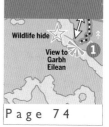

GETTING OUTSIDE IN FORT WILLIAM, GLEN COE AND LOCHABER

66 99

routes in this guide give a taste of some wild and remote country on safe, carefully selected short walks

OS Champion
Bee Leask

Ariundle Oakwood National Nature Reserve

A very warm welcome to the new Short Walks Made Easy guide to Fort William, Glen Coe and Lochaber – what a fantastic selection of leisurely walks we have for you!

Covering an area of the Highlands from Mallaig, on the west coast, to the Great Glen, and extending to the shore of Loch Sunart, deep into the West Highland Peninsulas, the routes in this guide give a taste of some wild and remote country on safe, carefully selected short walks.

Fort William is the hub of the region and a great base from which to explore on foot. Here you can stroll to the original eponymous fort and Inverlochy Castle. Linking Banavie and Corpach, a towpath walk along the Caledonian Canal passes the engineering marvel of Neptune's Staircase, with wonderful views to Ben Nevis; these can be admired closer to in the Glen Nevis ramble, which also is the starting point of the hike to Britain's highest peak.

The walk at Spean Bridge begins from the emotive Commando Memorial viewpoint; General Wade's High Bridge is a historic highlight. At Glenfinnan, there are truly breathtaking panoramas over the famous viaduct and down the length of Loch Shiel. For film buffs, there are Harry Potter movie locations, those from *Skyfall* in Glen Coe, and those from *Local Hero* at the most beautiful beach in the world, Camusdarach. The magically, atmospheric Atlantic oakwoods bring a sense of calm and wildlife-watching opportunities at Ariundle and Garbh Eilean.

Bee Leask, OS Champion

WE SMILE MORE
WHEN WE'RE OUTSIDE

Glencoe Lochan

Whether it's a short walk during our lunch break or a full day's outdoor adventure, we know that a good dose of fresh air is just the tonic we all need.

At Ordnance Survey (OS), we're passionate about helping more people to get outside more often. It sits at the heart of everything we do, and through our products and services, we aim to help you lead an active outdoor lifestyle, so that you can live longer, stay younger and enjoy life more.

We firmly believe the outdoors is for everyone, and we want to help you find the very best Great Britain has to offer. We are blessed with an island that is beautiful and unique, with a rich and varied landscape. There are coastal paths to meander along, woodlands to explore, countryside to roam, and cities to uncover. Our trusted source of inspirational content is bursting with ideas for places to go, things to do and easy beginner's guides on how to get started.

It can be daunting when you're new to something, so we want to bring you the know-how from the people who live and breathe the outdoors. To help guide us, our team of awe-inspiring OS Champions share their favourite places to visit, hints and tips for outdoor adventures, as well as tried and tested accessible, family- and wheelchair-friendly routes. We hope that you will feel inspired to spend more time outside and reap the physical and mental health benefits that the outdoors has to offer. With our handy guides, paper and digital mapping, and exciting new apps, we can be with you every step of the way.

To find out more visit os.uk/getoutside

RESPECTING
THE COUNTRYSIDE

You can't beat getting outside in the Scottish countryside, but it's vital that we leave no trace when we're enjoying the great outdoors.

Let's make sure that generations to come can enjoy the countryside just as we do.

 Care for your environment

 Keep your dog under proper control

 Take responsibility for your own actions

 Respect people's privacy and peace of mind

 Take extra care if organising a group or event

 Help land managers and others to work safely and effectively

For more details please visit
outdooraccess-scotland.scot

USING THIS GUIDE

Easy-to-follow Fort William, Glen Coe and Lochaber walks for all

Before setting off

Check the walk information panel to plan your outing

- Consider using **Public transport** where flagged. If driving, note the satnav postcode for the car park under **Parking**
- The suggested **Time** is based on a gentle pace
- Note the availability of **Cafés**, tearooms and pubs, and **Toilets**

Terrain and hilliness

- **Terrain** indicates the nature of the route surface
- Any rises and falls are noted under **Hilliness**

Walking with your dog?

- This panel states where **Dogs** must be on a lead and how many stiles there are – in case you need to lift your dog
- Keep dogs on leads where there are livestock and between April and August in forest and on moorland where there are ground-nesting birds

A perfectly pocket-sized walking guide

- Handily sized for ease of use on each walk
- When not being read, it fits nicely into a pocket...
- ...so between points, put this book in the pocket of your coat, trousers or day sack and enjoy your stroll in glorious countryside – we've made it pocket-sized for a reason!

Flexibility of route presentation to suit all readers

- **Not comfortable map reading?** Then use the simple-to-follow route profile and accompanying route description and pictures
- **Happy to map read?** New-look walk mapping makes it easier for you to focus on the route and the points of interest along the way
- **Read the insightful Did you know?, Local legend, Stories behind the walk** and **Nature notes** to help you make the most of your day out and to enjoy all that each walk has to offer

OS information about the walk

• Many of the features and symbols shown are taken from Ordnance Survey's celebrated **Explorer** mapping, designed to help people across Great Britain enjoy leisure time spent outside

• National Grid reference for the start point

• Explorer sheet map covering the route

OS information

🅰 NM 664917
Explorer 398

The easy-to-use walk map

• **Large-scale** mapping for ultra-clear route finding

• **Numbered points** at key turns along the route that tie in with the route instructions and respective points marked on the profile

• **Pictorial symbols** for intuitive map reading, see Map Symbols on the front cover flap

The simple-to-follow walk profile

• Progress easily along the route using the illustrative profile, it has **numbered points** for key turning points and **graduated distance** markers

• Easy-read **route directions** with turn-by-turn detail

• Reassuring **route photographs** for each numbered point

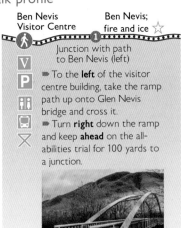

Using QR codes

- Scan each QR code to see the route in Ordnance Survey's OS Maps App.
NB You may need to download a scanning app if you have an older phone

- OS Maps will open the route automatically if you have it installed. If not, the route will open in the web version of OS Maps

- Please click **Start Route** button to begin navigating or **Download Route** to store the route for offline use

CAMUSDARACH BEACH, MORAR

Often cited as one of the most beautiful beaches in Scotland – or the whole world – Camusdarach has a special atmosphere. Lying just south of the Silver Sands of Morar, this stretch of coastline has been sculpted into a series of shallow bays where white sand shades into turquoise water. Rocky headlands separate these beaches, some little visited. An array of islands on the horizon enhance the view. Facing west, the main Camusdarach Beach is a fine place to watch the sunset.

OS information

🚶 NM 664917
Explorer 398

Distance
2.6 miles/4.2km

Time
1½ hours

Start/Finish
Camusdarach Beach car park

Parking PH40 4PD
Camusdarach Beach car park, on B8008 1½ miles west of junction with A830

Public toilets
Nearest: Morar Beach car park, ½ mile off A830 (summer); or West Bay car park, Mallaig

Cafés/pubs
Nearest in Morar

Terrain
Grass and earth paths; dunes and sandy beaches; gravel tracks

Hilliness
Gently undulating with brief ascents and descents to/from beaches

Footwear
Winter 🥾
Spring/Summer/ Autumn 👟

Did you know? Camusdarach Beach was a major location for filming the cult classic *Local Hero* (1983). Although the village that featured as fictional Ferness was Pennan in Aberdeenshire, Camusdarach was used as the beach owned by Ben, who lived in a shack on the shore. In the comedy-drama, Ben played a pivotal role in stopping an American corporation from building an oil refinery here.

Local legend Loch Morar, the deepest loch in Britain (with a maximum depth exceeding 1,000 feet), lies two miles inland from this walk. Its dark waters hide the monster Morag, less well known than Nessie but with many reported sightings. Two local men accidentally struck Morag with their boat, prompting her to attack them. Fended off with oar and rifle, the brown, 30-foot-long creature with three humps sank back below the surface.

STORIES BEHIND THE WALK

☆ **Camusdarach Beach** The stunning white sand of Camusdarach Beach is made up of the shells of sea creatures, which have been broken down into small particles by the action of the sea. Forming part of an extensive beach and dune system, tides and winds deposit this sand on the beaches and blow it inland to form dunes. The sea appears turquoise where the sand extends under the water and dark blue where rocks lie.

🔆 **Small Isles**
The Small Isles are an archipelago in the Inner Hebrides, between Skye and Mull. The main islands in the group are: Rùm, Eigg, Muck and Canna, which is hidden behind the jagged peaks of Rùm. To the left, Eigg looks like a surfacing minke whale whose dorsal fin is the Sgurr of Eigg, a rocky cone formed by a lava flow. These islands are rich in birdlife, from burrowing Manx shearwaters to mighty white-tailed eagles.

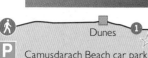

Kissir
gate

Gate 🔆
Small Isles
½ mile

2
3

Dunes **1**

☆ Camusdarach Beach

P Camusdarach Beach car park

➡ Exit the car park over the 'Footbridge to the Beaches' and then turn **right** by a green sign: Welcome to Camusdarach Beach.
➡ Walk under trees then descend through dunes and follow a stream to the beach.

1 ➡ Walk 350 yards to the end of the beach and turn **left** up wooden steps onto a deeply incised path then fork **left**.
➡ Pass a bench and climb steps to a wooden fence/gate.

☆ **Mallaig** The main settlement in the area is the village of Mallaig, which was founded as a fishing port in the 1840s by Lord Lovat, owner of North Morar Estate. Fishing is still an important part of the economy, but it is also a busy ferry port, with sailings to: the Small Isles; the Sleat peninsula at the south end of Skye; the remote peninsula of Knoydart; and South Uist in the Outer Hebrides. The route between Fort William and Mallaig is known as 'The Road to the Isles'.

☆ The Prince's Cairn

Ten miles south along the A830, on the shores of Loch nan Uamh, a cairn marks the spot where Bonnie Prince Charlie embarked for France after the failed Jacobite Rebellion of 1745. He had been on the run in the Hebrides for six months after a final and decisive defeat at the Battle of Culloden in April 1746. His supporters long hoped for his return, but it never happened.

1 mile

4
Wooden steps down to beach

5
Kissing-gate near a stone house

Gate pillars before road

➤ Go through the gate into a field.
➤ Bear **right** (up field), go through a kissing-gate at the top and turn **right** along a track to the corner of a high fence.

3 ➤ Turn **right** through a kissing-gate and follow the path to another gate above a small beach (wooden steps lead down to it).

4 ➤ Turn **left** (fence left) to reach a rusty-roofed boathouse and go through the gate beside it.
➤ Weave through rocky woodland then continue along the back of the next beach towards a stone house.

NATURE NOTES

Camusdarach and adjacent bays are part of a beach and dune system that runs along the west coast for about 6 miles from Arisaig to Mallaig. The beaches and dunes are formed of shell sand (see page 16).

Marram grass is important for stabilising the loose sand in the dunes. It is tolerant of salt spray and has spiky leaves.

Arctic terns are sometimes called 'sea swallows' because of their streamlined shape. They nest in colonies that they defend by swooping on intruders.

Gorse has coconut-scented yellow flowers and sharp, thorn-like leaves.

Blackface sheep graze the grassland behind the shore. The rams have heavy, curled horns.

Orange-tip butterflies have a distinctive camouflage pattern on their underwings. They feed on lady's smock and other wildflowers in spring.

Orange-tip

6 Gate | 1½ miles | **P** **7** Camusdarach Beach car park | **8** Path junction before a cream house

5 ➥ Turn **left**, go through a metal kissing-gate, and pass **left** of the house and up the drive.

➥ Just before gate pillars at the road, turn **left** on a track. Follow it for 500 yards, past **3**, to a gate into a field.

6 ➥ Turn **left** down the field, go through the bottom gate and turn **right** through a metal vehicle gate.

➥ Pass between old pines, descend through a metal gate and return over the footbridge to the car park.

Above: Artic tern
Below: Blackface ram

Top: marram grass
Above: shell sand
Below: gorse

Camusdarach Beach car park

House with
a grey roof

2 miles | **9** Dunes | 2½ miles | **P**

➡ From the car park entrance, turn **left** through a gate with a No Vehicles sign.
➡ Fork **left** below houses then fork **left** again to a path junction 40 yards before a cream house.

8 ➡ At the junction, turn **right** on a grassy path that turns sandy as it rises over dunes.
➡ Keep **left** to meet the beach then turn **right** along it to the far end.

9 ➡ In front of rocks, turn **right** through dunes then keep **ahead**, aiming just **right** of a house with a grey roof.
➡ Pass below the house, turn **right** down its drive and follow the track back to the car park.

GO BY TRAIN
CATCH A BUS

GLENFINNAN

Set between high mountains at the head of Loch Shiel, Glenfinnan has two main claims to fame: the spectacular Glenfinnan Viaduct and the Glenfinnan Monument, which marks the start of the Second Jacobite Rebellion. Its history is described in the National Trust for Scotland (NTS) Visitor Centre. Half of this route is on flat ground around the River Finnan, while the more energetic half follows the Viaduct Trail for a bird's-eye view of the railway and loch.

OS information

NM 906807
Explorer 398

Distance
3 miles/4.75 km

Time
1¾ hours

Start/Finish
Glenfinnan

Parking PH37 4LT
Glenfinnan
Community car park

Public toilets
At the NTS Visitor
Centre

Cafés/pubs
NTS Viaduct
View Café and
Visitor Centre
café; Glenfinnan
Station Dining Car;
Glenfinnan House
Hotel

Terrain
Surfaced and
unsurfaced paths,
with stone steps and
boardwalk; pavement
and lanes

Hilliness
Fairly level below the
railway line but a
steep ascent and
descent on the
Viaduct Trail ❶ to
❹

Footwear
Winter 👢
Spring/Summer/
Autumn 👟

Public transport

Train services to Glenfinnan Station (joining the walk ❹ to ❺): scotrail.co.uk. Bus stops on the A830 near Glenfinnan Station and near ⓧ for services 500/501 between Mallaig and Lochailort: shielbuses.co.uk

Accessibility
••••••••••••

Wheelchair and pushchair friendly ⓧ to ❶, and then to complete a circuit, use drive ❶ to ❻, then pavement to ❾ and path to the monument at ❽

Dogs

Welcome but keep on leads by A830. No stiles

Did you know? Glenfinnan is a tourist hotspot, especially in summer, so parking is at a premium. The NTS Visitor Centre car park fills up quickly, so the local community set up a charitable trust to raise funds and build another larger car park, as well as to undertake other infrastructure projects. This car park is where the walk starts, but to secure a place arrive early! Or arrive by train or bus.

Local legend Reputedly, a horse fell into one of the piers during construction of the Glenfinnan Viaduct. In 1987, a fisheye camera was lowered into the largest pier, but nothing was found. However, rumours suggested the accident may actually have occurred at the Loch nan Uamh Viaduct over the A830, 14 miles west. In 2001, scanning technology was used on that viaduct and the remains of the horse and cart were found within the large central pier.

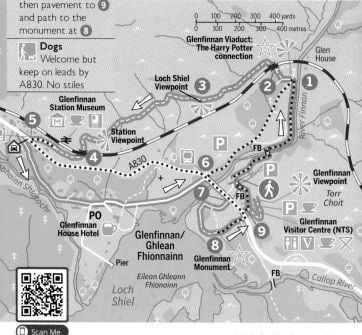

STORIES BEHIND THE WALK

☆ **Glenfinnan Monument** The 59-foot-high tower on the shore of Loch Shiel marks the spot where Bonnie Prince Charlie rallied the clans on 19 August 1745. He had recently arrived from exile in France and was gathering support to overthrow the Hanoverian monarchy, and reinstate the Stuarts. The statue of an unknown Highlander at the top commemorates all those who lost their lives in this failed Jacobite Rebellion. Tickets to climb the monument should be booked in advance via the NTS website (nts.org.uk).

🏛 **Glenfinnan Station Museum** A charitable trust was set up in 1991 to save Glenfinnan Station and retain it as a stop on the railway line. The museum exhibition describes how the spectacular railway was built. The Dining Car serves home baking and light lunches, and the Sleeping Car has been converted into a well-equipped bunkhouse. Allow time to explore the station and visit the signal box and gift shop (glenfinnanstation museum.co.uk).

Glen Road Viewpoint

Glenfinnan Viaduct; the Harry Potter connection ☆

River Finnan footbridge

Glenfinnan Community car park

❶ ½ mile Pass under the viaduct

➡ Walk to the far end of the car park, under two height barriers, towards the viaduct as signed.
➡ Cross a footbridge (River Finnan) and turn **right** along a riverside path for ¼ mile to a crossways.

❶ ➡ Turn **left** along the track for the accessible road circuit (see map).
➡ Otherwise, keep **ahead** on a rising path, signed Station Museum and Viaduct Trail.
➡ Soon pass Glen Road Viewpoint and climb to the viaduct.

☆ The Harry Potter Connection

Many photographers position themselves to catch the morning or afternoon train service crossing the viaduct. In summer, *The Jacobite*, a steam locomotive-hauled tourist train, operates from Fort William to Mallaig. It has featured on the Glenfinnan Viaduct and stopping at Glenfinnan Station in several films, most famously four of the Harry Potter films, where it was the *Hogwarts Express*.

☆ Glenfinnan Viaduct

The famous Glenfinnan Viaduct carries the West Highland Line from Fort William to Mallaig. Completed in 1898, it is the longest concrete railway bridge in Scotland at 416 yards, and crosses the River Finnan at a height of 100 feet. The viaduct has 21 semi-circular spans of 50 feet and has featured on the Bank of Scotland £10 note.

Loch Shiel Viewpoint · 1 mile · Station Viewpoint ☀ · Pass under the railway · Glenfinnan Station Museum 🏛 🍵

② ➡ Pass under the viaduct, go through a weighted wooden gate, rising to the Viaduct Viewpoint.
➡ Here, the path bends **left** along the hillside, with boardwalk and steps to the next viewpoint in ¼ mile.

③ ➡ This is the Loch Shiel Viewpoint. Continue on the path, which dips down then rises behind a small plantation.
➡ At the Station Viewpoint, the path turns **right**, downhill, then curves **left** down to the railway line.

④ ➡ Go through a gate, under the railway, down steps across a miniature railway and over a footbridge.
➡ Steps lead to the station, museum, shop and dining car. After visiting, go down Station Road to the A830.

NATURE NOTES

Loch Shiel is a 17-mile-long freshwater lake that runs between Glenfinnan and Acharacle (near Walk 10). It is enclosed by wild mountains and has no roads down its length, but you can explore it with Loch Shiel Cruises. Both golden and white-tailed eagles are often seen from the boat, as well as osprey, black-throated diver and other wildlife.

The open hillsides around Glenfinnan have plants characteristic of Highland moorlands. The damp, peaty ground is ideal for wildflowers such as bog asphodel, whose bright yellow flower stalks grow in wetter patches. The acid habitat also favours the heath spotted orchid, which grows prolifically through the rough grasses.

Look out on the Viaduct Trail for the Scotch argus butterfly, which is only found in the north-west Highlands. On sunny days in July and August, the males fly almost without rest, weaving low through the grass in search of females.

The wooded areas lower down have wildflowers that like richer soils and are shade tolerant, such as bugle and lesser celandine.

Loch S

1½ miles

Glenfinnan House Hotel

A830

2 miles

5 ⮕ **Cross** the main road and turn **right** along the pavement.
⮕ In 50 yards, go **left** onto a track.
⮕ Continue for ⅓ mile to meet a lane; bear **left**, following it for another ⅓ mile past Glenfinnan House Hotel to the A830.

6 ⮕ At the main road, turn along the pavement and over the River Finnan.
⮕ Pass the car park entrance then turn **right** down a track to a pedestrian gate beside a vehicle gate.

7 ⮕ Go through the pedestrian gate then bear **right** on a gravel track to a T-junction at the far end.
⮕ Turn **left** towards Loch Shiel, following the track as it curves **left** to the Glenfinnan Monument.

Top left: lesser celandine
Above: spotted orchid
Top right: bog asphodel

Scotch argus

Glenfinnan Monument ☆

Glenfinnan Visitor Centre (NTS)

Glenfinnan Visitor Centre (NTS)

Glenfinnan Viewpoint

V ☕

7
30

8
2½ miles

9

V ☕

NTS car park; Viaduct View Café

3 miles

Glenfinnan Community car park

8 ➡ Turn **left** at the monument onto a tarmac path to the road.
➡ **Cross** carefully to the NTS Visitor Centre and keep to the **left** side of the building to a Glenfinnan Viewpoint sign.

9 ➡ Follow the signed arrow and climb to the viewpoint.
➡ Return down the path; turn **right** through the NTS car park to Viaduct View Café, there turning **left** over a footbridge back to the start.

Walk 2 Glenfinnan **25**

This page (clockwise): Mamore Mountains, Kinlochleven; Ben Nevis from Corpach picnic area; Tailrace from the hydroelectric plant, Fort William; Garbh Eilean wildlife hide, Loch Sunart

Opposite (clockwise): Commando Memorial, Spean Bridge; River Nevis; River Coe, Glen Coe

27

SPEAN BRIDGE

This walk lies 10 miles up the Great Glen from Fort William. It follows a well-made path, starting from the evocative Commando Memorial. From here you can enjoy an amazing panorama of mountains, including Ben Nevis and the ski slopes of Aonach Mòr. Two historic routes traversed this landscape: General Wade's military road, which crossed the River Spean by the High Bridge, and a disused railway, followed here for ½ mile through wildlife-rich native woodland.

OS information

🧭 NN 207824
Explorer 400

Distance
3.25 miles/5.2km

Time
1¾ hours

Start/Finish
Commando Memorial, Spean Bridge

Parking PH34 4EG
Commando Memorial car park

Public toilets
Nearest: Mill toilets, Spean Bridge Woollen Mill, PH34 4EP (0.3 mile from ❸, 1.3 miles from 🧭)

Cafés/pubs
Nearest in Spean Bridge

Terrain
Surfaced paths and pavement

Hilliness
Gradual descent ❶ to ❹ then steady climb back to 🧭 from ❼

Footwear
Year round 👢

Did you know? The first shots of the 1745 Jacobite rising were fired at Spean Bridge. Called the Highbridge Skirmish, 11 MacDonell clansmen fooled a company of 80 government troops into thinking that the bridge was heavily defended. The soldiers retreated and were pursued up the Great Glen, where they met MacDonell reinforcements and surrendered. Emboldened by this success, Bonnie Prince Charlie's standard was raised at Glenfinnan three days later and his campaign was launched (see Walk 2).

Local legend This walk is situated in the heart of Clan Cameron's ancestral lands. According to legend, they are descended from a Danish prince who helped King Fergus II of Scotland reclaim his throne in the 6th century. He was nicknamed Cameron for his crooked nose – cam-shròn in Scottish Gaelic. The current chief resides at Achnacarry Castle, 5 miles to the west, where the Clan Cameron Museum occupies an estate cottage.

Public transport

Train services to Spean Bridge Station (½ mile from **8**): scotrail.co.uk. Bus stop on the A82 (at Spean Crescent, 0.4 mile from **8**) for services 919 between Inverness and Fort William: citylink.co.uk; and N41, between Fort William and Roybridge: shielbuses. co.uk

Accessibility

Powered wheelchairs around the memorial and from **8** to end; route suitable for pushchairs but two kissing-gates at **1** and **8**

Dogs

Welcome but keep on leads beside the A82. No stiles

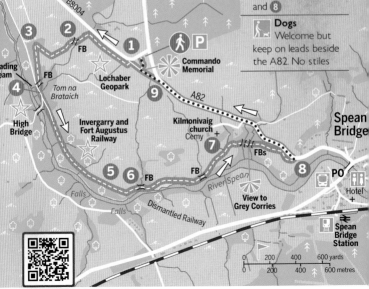

STORIES BEHIND THE WALK

☆ **High Bridge** General Wade, who was charged with controlling the Highlanders after the first Jacobite uprising in 1715, constructed 250 miles of military roads. Built in 1736, High Bridge – at over 80 feet – was the highest of 40 bridges he erected. It

formed an important link between the garrisons at Fort William, Fort Augustus and Inverness. By 1819 it was crumbling and Thomas Telford designed a replacement, half a mile downstream, after which the village of Spean Bridge was named.

✳ Commando Memorial

The environs of this walk were part of the training area for Commandos based at Achnacarry during World War II. After the war, ideas were invited for a memorial to all Commandos who died fighting for their country. A bronze statue of three figures designed by a teacher from Dundee College of Art was chosen. It was unveiled here by Queen Elizabeth the Queen Mother in 1952.

☆ Lochaber Geopark

 ✳ Commando Memorial

1 Wooden kissing-gate

2 Footbridge ¦ ½ mile

3

P Commando Memorial car park

➥ From the car park's top corner, walk up to the Commando Memorial and viewpoint indicator.
➥ Keep **ahead** down steps to a lane and turn **right** along it for 150 yards to a wooden kissing-gate.

1 ➥ Turn **left** to go through the kissing-gate (fingerpost signed Spean Bridge via historic High Bridge).
➥ Walk parallel to the B8004, past two information boards, bending **left** opposite Old Pines Hotel down to a footbridge.

2 ➥ **Cross** the footbridge and continue downhill towards young pine trees.
➥ Beyond the pines the path curves **right**, down into birch woodland, to reach a sharp **left** bend.

☆ **Invergarry and Fort Augustus Railway** From **6** you can view the 76-foot-high concrete piers of a railway viaduct over the River Spean. It was one of two viaducts built to serve the Invergarry and Fort Augustus Railway, which opened in 1903. Its investors hoped to link to Inverness through the Great Glen, but it only connected to a pier at Fort Augustus, from where steam boats continued up Loch Ness. The line never made money and closed in 1946.

☆ **Lochaber Geopark**

An information board near **1** describes the geological processes that formed the mountains of the Nevis Range and Grey Corries, which together fill the skyline to the south. It explains how Ben Nevis is the root of an extinct volcano and why the Grey Corries shine with white quartzite. This is one of several boards around Lochaber Geopark, which covers the same region as this book.

View of cascades
(right, 50 yards)

4 Footbridge ☆ 1 mile ☆ **I n v e r g a r r y   a n d   F o r t   A u g u s t u s   R a i l w a y**

High Bridge (information board)

1½ miles

Fork **5**   Footbridge **6**

Dismantled bridge piers and Steam up the Glen (information board)

---

3 ➡ Carry on round the bend and descend to the old railway line, crossing a footbridge just before it.
➡ (Go 50 yards **right** to view an old railway bridge over the cascading stream just crossed.)

4 ➡ Turn **left** along the old track bed, immediately crossing a smaller stream.
➡ In 100 yards, there's a view of ruined High Bridge from an information board. Continue high above the River Spean to a fork in ½ mile.

NATURE NOTES

The Commando Memorial has wonderful all-round views. On cloudless nights in the darker months it is a good place to look for the Northern Lights, if solar activity is forecast. No towns or street lights lie to the north to spoil the wondrous sight of curtains and beams of green, red and purple light illuminating the sky.

Birch is a relatively short-lived tree that grows well on poor soils and improves the ground for other species, such as oak, to colonise.

Wood anemones are adapted to growing under deciduous trees and flower early, before they become shaded by the woodland canopy.

The mix of wood and rough open land is the favourite habit of roe deer.

In summer, look out on the sunny, open slopes above the River Spean for meadow brown butterflies.

The varied tree and grassland habitats around Spean Bridge are home to one of the most north-westerly barn owl populations in Britain.

Birch

2 miles · ⑦ · View to Grey Corries

Footbridge · Bench · Footbridge · Kissing gate

⑤ ▪ Fork **left** off the old railway line 175 yards before a fence across a dismantled bridge over the river.
▪ Bend **left** with the path over a footbridge beside the bridge piers to an information board: Steam up the Glen.

⑥ ▪ Cross open land then re-enter woodland over a footbridge.
▪ Pass lovely mature oak trees beside the river, cross another footbridge then rise up an open area for 250 yards to a bench.

Top left: wood anemone
Top right: Northern Lights
Above: meadow brown

Roe deer

Commando
Memorial

Kilmonivaig church

2½ miles

Brown signs

3 miles

A 8 2   p a v e m e n t

Commando
Memorial
car park

7 ➡ Pass the bench under a magnificent oak, pausing for a mountain view.
➡ The path climbs more then winds round the hillside, crossing two footbridges, with a view to Grey Corries before reaching a main road.

8 ➡ Go through the kissing-gate and turn **left** up the pavement, continuing to brown tourist signs in ¾ mile, passing Kilmonivaig church on the way.

9 ➡ Reaching the brown signs, bear **left** away from the main road towards the memorial.
➡ Branch **right** past the statue to return to the car park.

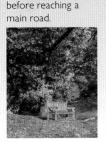

CALEDONIAN CANAL

Linking the communities of Banavie and Corpach, this flat walk follows towpaths on either side of the Caledonian Canal. It covers its southern stretch, between the sea at Loch Linnhe and the amazing engineering feat of Neptune's Staircase. Ben Nevis is visible throughout the route, but looks particularly impressive from the picnic site at Corpach. Allow time to stop and watch yachts traversing the locks – it's a fascinating sight. The road and rail swing bridges may also open to let boats through.

OS information

🚶 NN 112769
Explorer 399

Distance
3.2 miles / 5.1 km

Time
1¾ hours

Start/Finish
Banavie

Parking PH33 7PL
Neptune's Staircase car park

Public toilets
Kilmallie Hall, Corpach, close to ④; Caol Shopping Centre, Caol, ⅓ mile from ⑥

Cafés/pubs
The Moorings Hotel, Banavie, between ⑨ and 🚶; An Cafaidh Mara at Corpach Marina, near ④

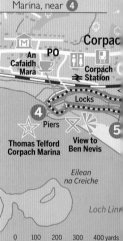

Corpach

An Cafaidh Mara • PO

Corpach Station

Locks

④ Piers

Thomas Telford Corpach Marina

View to Ben Nevis ⑤

Eilean na Creiche

Loch Linnhe

| 0 | 100 | 200 | 300 | 400 yards |
| 0 | 100 | 200 | 300 | 400 metres |

Did you know? Saint Patrick, the patron saint of Ireland, may have been born at Banavie, around CE 389. He wrote that his birthplace was in Britain at a place he called 'Bannavem Taburniae'. When he was 16 years old pirates kidnapped him and took him to Ireland as a slave. In his 20s, he escaped and returned home before training as a cleric. He returned to Ireland as a missionary and converted thousands to Christianity.

Local legend The construction of the Caledonian Canal was foreseen in 1620 by a Highland prophet called the Brahan Seer. He predicted that one day full-rigged ships would sail round the back of Tomnahurich, a hill near Inverness. At the time it was thought to be impossible because the only waterway was the River Ness, which flowed on the other side of the hill.

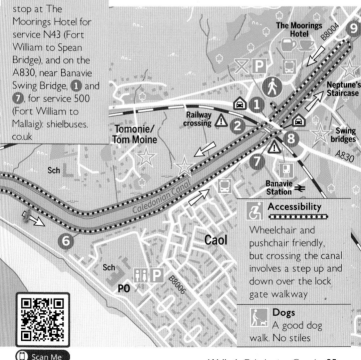

Accessibility
Wheelchair and pushchair friendly, but crossing the canal involves a step up and down over the lock gate walkway

Dogs
A good dog walk. No stiles

Scan Me

STORIES BEHIND THE WALK

☆ Caledonian Canal

Opened in 1822, the Caledonian Canal provides a safe route between east and west coasts, avoiding dangerous seas around northern Scotland. The 18-foot-wide canal links lochs strung along the Great Glen, a deep valley following a fault line between Fort William and Inverness. It took 21 years to complete, by which time many of the new, iron-hulled ships of the period were too large for it.

☆ Neptune's Staircase

This walk finishes beside a flight of eight locks that form the longest staircase loc in Britain. Named after the Roman god of the sea, Neptune's Staircase lifts and lowers boa 64 feet in the space 500 yards. Originally operated by hand, it took over half a day to transit the syste Now, converted to push-button hydrau operation, the passa takes about 90 minutes.

A830 ☆ **Swing bridges**   ☆ Tom Moine   ½ mile

🚶 ❶❷ ▪▪▪▪▪▪▪▪▪▪▪▪▪▪▪▪▪▪▪▪▪▪▪▪▪▪▪▪▪▪▪▪▪▪▪▪▪▪

P   ⚠ 🏠 Banavie Station

✗   ☆ C A L E D O N I A N   C a n a l

Neptune's taircase ar park

➡ Leave the car park on a gravel track at its far end by a sign: Caledonian Canal.
➡ Turn **right** at a T-junction along the canal towpath for 50 yards to reach the main road.

❶ ➡ **Cross** the A830 with care.
➡ In 35 yards, come to a railway crossing with kissing-gates on both sides (and wider wheelchair gates).

❷ ➡ Carefully **cross** the railway.
➡ Pass a bench with a view of the Lock Keeper's Cottage and Ben Nevis then follow the towpath **ahead** through countryside for almost 1 mile to Corpach Double Lock.

☆ **Swing bridges** The canal was designed for, and is still used by, sailing boats with tall masts. As the landscape doesn't lend itself to high bridges, cars and trains crossing it use swing bridges that can be opened to allow for the passage of boats. At Banvie, the West Coast railway line and A830 road swing bridges are side by side, the latter controlled by traffic lights.

☆ **Thomas Telford Corpach Marina** Scotland's newest marina is named after Thomas Telford, who designed the Caledonian Canal. It is situated by the white lighthouse marking the entrance to Corpach Sea Lock and has berths for up to 45 yachts and motor vessels. Facilities include a coffee shop, An Cafaidh Mara, and car park. It operates as an independent business, community owned by Caol Regeneration Company (corpachmarina.co.uk).

| Corpach Double Lock | An Cafaidh Mara | **Thomas Telford Corpach Marina** P ☕ ☆ | View to ⚘ Ben Nevis |

☆ **C a l e d o n i a n   C a n a l**

1 mile   Corpach Station (right)   1½ miles   Corpach Double Lock

Corpach Sea Lock

♿ Step up/down at lock crossing

3 ➡ Pass through an open gateway to the loch, where the path dips to a wide canal basin.
➡ Walk beside the canal, through a car park, to Corpach Sea Lock. Turn **left** over the last lock gate before the sea.

4 ➡ Turn **left** again through a wooden gate, up the other side of the canal.
➡ Pass a grassy picnic area, with a splendid view of Ben Nevis and the canal basin, to Corpach Double Lock.

NATURE NOTES

Land, freshwater and marine habitats are encountered on this walk, so a wide range of species may be seen. Tom Moine, the wetland on the right after crossing the railway line at ②, supports many wildflowers that grow near water, such as water avens.

Damp grassland is also a likely place to see green-veined white butterflies. The markings on their underwings distinguish them from the 'cabbage whites'.

The mown grass fringing the canal is dotted with short-growing wildflowers, including daisy, dandelion and pretty, blue germander speedwell.

The canal basin at Corpach is home to mute swans and mallards, which will swim towards you if they think you have food.

From the picnic site by Corpach Sea Lock, you are looking out over Loch Linnhe, the enclosed arm of seawater that angles south at Fort William and runs between mountains towards the Inner Hebrides. The large tidal range here means that sea anemones and other creatures living underwater are sometimes exposed.

Sea anemones

Path junction/
blue sign | 2 miles

⑥

☆ Caledonian Canal

⑤ ➡ By the lock, keep **left** at a blue sign for Banavie.
➡ Follow the towpath up past the lock and over a weir. Continue for ¼ mile to a path junction at a blue Caol/Fort William sign.

⑥ ➡ At the junction, keep **ahead** beside the canal.
➡ Continue for ½ mile to the railway line.

⑦ ➡ Again, **cross** with care, going through both kissing-gates.
➡ To the **right** of the station entrance, **cross** the main road carefully on a marked footpath/cycle route and go **left**.

Top: mallard Bottom: mute swan

Above: germander speedwell
Below: water avens

♿ Step up/down at lock crossing

Railway crossing
Swing bridges

miles ⚠️

Banavie Station
Bottom lock

9
Top lock

3 miles ☕

**N e p t u n e ' s
S t a i r c a s e**

☆ **C a l e d o n i a n   C a n a l**

The Moorings Hotel

Bottom lock

🅿️

Neptune's Staircase car park

8 ➡ Walk past the bridge control building back onto the towpath.
➡ For a shortcut, cross the first lock gate back to **Ⓧ**.
➡ Otherwise, rise with the towpath beside Neptune's Staircase to the top.

9 ➡ **Cross** the top lock gate and turn **left** back down the canal towpath.
➡ Return past The Moorings Hotel and, before the A830, turn **right** back into the car park.

Opposite (clockwise): barn owl; alder catkins; roe deer
This page (clockwise): green-veined white; Silver Sands, Morar; herring gull; moss, Ariundle Oakwood National Nature Reserve

FORT WILLIAM

This level walk links two ruined fortifications: the Old Fort on the shore of Loch Linnhe and Inverlochy Castle, overlooking the River Lochy. Both are well interpreted with information boards. The walk heads out of Fort William along the first part of the Great Glen Way, a long-distance route marked with thistle symbols running to Inverness. From the busy town centre it soon leads into riverside woodland then tranquil countryside, with views of Ben Nevis. The return is through Inverlochy village.

OS information

NN 107743
Explorer 392

Distance
3.2 mile/5.1km

Time
1¾ hours

Start/Finish
An-Aird, Fort William

Parking PH33 6EW
An-Aird No. 1 car park

Public toilets
Travel Centre, Station Square, Fort William PH33 6DZ

Cafés/pubs
Larder Café at the Highland Soap Company Visitor Centre, near ⑦; Fort William

Terrain
Tarmac and grass paths; pavement and lanes

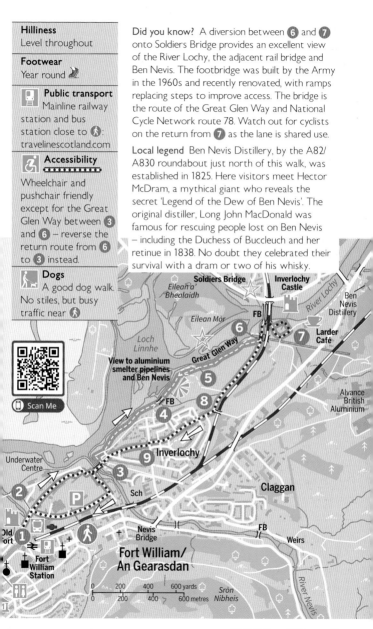

Hilliness
Level throughout

Footwear
Year round

Public transport
Mainline railway station and bus station close to 🚶:
travelinescotland.com

Accessibility
Wheelchair and pushchair friendly except for the Great Glen Way between ③ and ⑥ – reverse the return route from ⑥ to ③ instead.

Dogs
A good dog walk. No stiles, but busy traffic near 🚶

Did you know? A diversion between ⑥ and ⑦ onto Soldiers Bridge provides an excellent view of the River Lochy, the adjacent rail bridge and Ben Nevis. The footbridge was built by the Army in the 1960s and recently renovated, with ramps replacing steps to improve access. The bridge is the route of the Great Glen Way and National Cycle Network route 78. Watch out for cyclists on the return from ⑦ as the lane is shared use.

Local legend Ben Nevis Distillery, by the A82/A830 roundabout just north of this walk, was established in 1825. Here visitors meet Hector McDram, a mythical giant who reveals the secret 'Legend of the Dew of Ben Nevis'. The original distiller, Long John MacDonald was famous for rescuing people lost on Ben Nevis – including the Duchess of Buccleuch and her retinue in 1838. No doubt they celebrated their survival with a dram or two of his whisky.

Scan Me

STORIES BEHIND THE WALK

🏰 **Old Fort** Fort William was named after the fort whose remains are at ❶. It was constructed on the command of King William of Orange in 1690. The stone walls were 20 feet high and encompassed a large area, including the present site of the railway station. The fort housed 1,000 soldiers charged with controlling

the Highlands and stopping Jacobites from restoring the Stuart monarchy. In 1692, orders for the infamous Massacre of Glencoe (Walk 8) were issued from here.

☆ **Great Glen Way** The site of the Old Fort at ❶ is the official western terminus for the Great Glen Way, a 73-mile route exploring Scotland's longest glen. It can be tackled in part or in one go, on foot, by bike or by boat, with variations for each mode of travel. This walk follows the first 1½ miles of the route, which then heads west to join the Caledonian Canal (Walk 4).

Old Fort

🏰 🚻 ☆ **G r e a t   G l e n   W a y**

An-Aird roundabout

❶   ❷   ❸

🚶 Morrisons (left) 🅿

An-Aird No. 1 car park

🍴 An-Aird roundabout

¦½ mile   River Nevis bridg

L o c

♿ See map for accessible route to

➡ From the car park, walk towards the An-Aird roundabout, passing Morrisons (left).

➡ At the roundabout's first exit, carefully cross to the Great Glen Way sign and turn left along the pavement for 30 yards.

❶ ➡ Enter the grassy picnic area, **right**, site of the Old Fort and a monolith marking the start of the Great Glen Way (GGW).

➡ Enjoy the ruins and information boards then return to An-Aird roundabout.

⚜ Aluminium smelter

After ④, you can see twin pipelines running down the flank of Ben Nevis to the hydro-powered aluminium smelter, owned by Alvance British Aluminium. A 15-mile tunnel under Ben Nevis brings water from Loch Treig and Loch Laggan. The energy created is used to convert bauxite into aluminium. Inverlochy village was purpose-built in the 1920s to house smelter workers. Look out for the statue of a furnace worker between ⑧ and ⑨.

View to aluminium smelter pipelines and Ben Nevis ⚜

🏰 Inverlochy Castle

Standing on the south bank of the River Lochy, Inverlochy Castle controlled the strategically important entrance to the Great Glen. It was built around 1275, during the reign of Alexander III of Scotland. Unusually, its structure has remained unaltered since it was built, though for much of that time it has been partially ruined. Two battles were fought here, in 1431 and 1645.

R i v e r   L o c h y

1 mile ┊ ④ Footbridge   ⑤ ④ ┊ 1½ miles

i n n h e   s h o r e   p a t h

▶ Take the second exit and walk to the **left** of McDonald's on a path signed Inverlochy, Caol and Corpach.
▶ At a T-junction, go **right** then **left** through housing to a bridge across the River Nevis.

③ ▶ **Cross** the bridge and turn immediately **left** on the GGW.
▶ Follow the blue posts with a thistle symbol along the Loch Linnhe shore. Keep **ahead** when a track joins from the right to a footbridge in ⅓ mile.

④ ▶ Go **over** the first of two bridges where horse riders are requested to dismount.
▶ Enter an open area (fine view to Ben Nevis and the pipes of the hydro-powered aluminium smelter running down the hillside), continuing to a pedestrian gate.

NATURE NOTES

This walk explores the woods, farmland and urban setting on the flat, fertile ground between Loch Linnhe and Ben Nevis, with the sea moderating the climate but the mountains increasing rainfall.

Sport anglers fish from the shore in the town, catching dogfish, thornback rays, flounder, whiting and sea trout.

At the Old Fort, and elsewhere along the seafront, you may see herring gulls. The adults have pink legs and a red spot on their heavy yellow bill. Young birds are mottled brown and take four years to reach maturity.

As you walk inland through the woods at the mouth of the River Lochy, you may see primroses in spring and wild raspberries in summer.

Small copper butterflies may be seen in the shorter grassland beside the river. Here, at the north-western limit of their range, they need sheltered, warm spots to feed on wildflowers.

Grassy areas on the edge of town are also inhabited by rabbits, whose digging has proved a nuisance on the shinty pitch, passed near the end of the walk.

Soldiers Bridge (River Lochy)   ☆   🏰 **Inverlochy Castle**   **Weak Bridge sign**   Metal-fenced electricty substa...

6   **7**   **8**

Weak Bridge sign

'2 miles

5 ➤ Pass through the gate and take to a narrower path beside the River Lochy, towards Soldiers Bridge.

➤ Beyond another pedestrian gate meet a tarmac lane.

6 ➤ Turn **left** past a Weak Bridge sign and at Soldiers Bridge turn **right** through an arch under the railway line.

➤ Bend **right** beside Inverlochy Castle then, in 100 yards, **left** to its archway entrance.

7 ➤ Walk through the castle ruins then turn **left**, back under the railway, returning to **6**.

➤ This time, continue **straight ahead** on a tarmac lane for ½ mile to a metal-fenced electricity substation.

Top: primroses
Middle: small copper
Bottom: dogfish

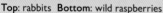

Top: rabbits Bottom: wild raspberries

2½ miles Furnace worker sculpture Wade Road River Nevis bridge 3 miles Playground An-Aird No. 1 car park

8 ➡ Keep **forward** as the path rises to a housing estate and, ignoring all side turnings, in ¼ mile pass a grassy triangle with a furnace worker sculpture.
➡ At a staggered crossroads (shops), go **left** then **right** into Wade Road.

9 ➡ Walk **ahead** on pavement to re-cross the River Nevis bridge.
➡ Go **left** at the next junction for 175 yards then turn **right** beyond a playground to return to the car park.

WALK 6

GLEN NEVIS

This route starts from the car park at the foot of Ben Nevis where most people begin their ascent. Instead of a long slog uphill to the summit of Britain's highest mountain, this walk follows a pretty, all-abilities path beside the River Nevis. After crossing the river to the youth hostel, it returns by forest tracks along the other side of the glen. That involves a short ascent and descent, but there is the option of walking back on the pavement beside the road.

OS information

🚶 NN 122729
Explorer 392

Distance
2.75 miles/4.4km

Time
1½ hours

Start/Finish
Ben Nevis Visitor Centre

Parking PH33 6ST
Glen Nevis Visitor Centre car park

Public toilets
Ben Nevis Visitor Centre

Cafés/pubs
No café but drinks/ snacks at the visitor centre; Glen Nevis Restaurant/Bar at **4**

Terrain
All-abilities path 🚶 to **3** then pavement to **4**; forest roads; narrow, steep woodland path

Hilliness
Level from 🚶 to **4**; gradual climb to the forest road at **6** and steeper descent to **8**

Footwear
Year round 👟

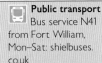
Did you know? From 1883 to 1904, a few hardy
individuals lived in a small stone hut on the summit
of Ben Nevis. Their shelter was built by the Scottish
Meteorological Society with the aim of taking hourly
recordings of the weather: wind speed, rainfall,
humidity and atmospheric pressure. The volunteers
who manned it all year round sometimes had to dig
themselves out of 5-foot snow drifts or struggle
against 100mph winds.

Local legend If you do this walk outside the
warmer months you may meet Cailleach Bheur,
the giant goddess of winter. Described as an old
hag with white hair and blue skin, she lays her
white shawl over Scotland's mountains in winter.
Millennia ago she strode across the country
creating islands and valleys, but her power waned
and now she has to rest during the summer.

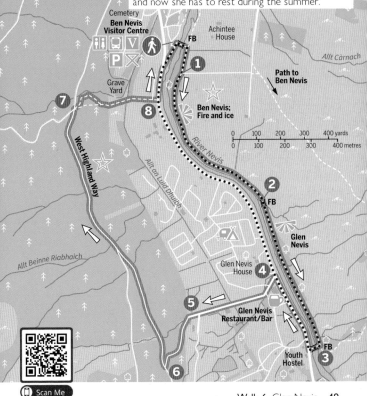

STORIES BEHIND THE WALK

☆ **Fire and ice** Cailleach Bheur may be the legendary creator of Scotland's landscapes, but geologists reveal that the cliffs of Ben Nevis were carved by glaciers. The mountain was formed 400 million years ago by a volcano that rose 2,000 feet higher than the current summit. The caldera collapsed in on itself leaving hard, solidified lava at its core. This now forms the summit, while the surrounding granite has been worn down by glacial action.

🌊 **Glen Nevis**
The public road runs for another 5 miles up the glen to a car park. From there a rocky path continues upriver through a dramatic gorge. The glen opens up again opposite the Steall Waterfall, the second highest in Britain, with a single drop of 390 feet. Both the falls and a hut used by mountaineering clubs lie on the far side of the river, only crossed by braving a commando-style wire bridge.

Ben Nevis Visitor Centre

Ben Nevis; fire and ice ☆ 🌊

½ mile | **Footbridge**

① Junction with path to Ben Nevis (left)

View (left) to Ben Nevis and climbers on the path to the summit

② Glen N

View up the

🚶 Ⓥ Ⓟ 🚻 🚌 ✕

🔹 To the **left** of the visitor centre building, take the ramp path up onto Glen Nevis bridge and cross it.
🔹 Turn **right** down the ramp and keep **ahead** on the all-abilities trial for 100 yards to a junction.

① 🔹 At the junction, where the Ben Nevis path goes left uphill, bear **right** by the river, passing a picnic table (after which, look left to spot walkers beginning the Ben Nevis climb).
🔹 In ⅓ mile meet a footbridge.

☆ West Highland Way

This walk follows part of the final leg of the West Highland Way, which terminates in Fort William. One of the most famous of Britain's long-distance routes, it is 96 miles long and starts just north of Glasgow. Backpackers you meet may be looking weary after crossing the mountains from Kinlochleven (Walk 7). The previous day they will have tackled the infamous Devil's Staircase out of the head of Glen Coe.

🔆 Ben Nevis

Ben Nevis towers 4,406 feet above Fort William on the shores of Loch Linnhe, rising from sea level to summit in a short distance. The Ben Nevis Visitor Centre has an altitude of only 50 feet, so it's a long climb to the top! Nevertheless, over 120,000 people ascend it each year and some hardy souls compete in the gruelling Ben Nevis Race. Unbelievably, the record for running up and down (set in 1984) is 1 hour 25 minutes 34 seconds.

Footbridge, River Nevis ¦ 1 mile

Youth hostel

Glen Nevis Resturant/Bar

2 ➡ Go over the footbridge and pass another picnic table then a bench, with a lovely view up the glen.

➡ Beyond a third picnic table, the path makes a wide curve between fences to a bridge.

3 ➡ Turn **right** to cross the footbridge over the River Nevis, go down a ramp and cross the road to the youth hostel.

➡ Turn **right** along the pavement for 300 yards to Glen Nevis Restaurant/Bar.

4 ➡ Turn **left** off the road onto the restaurant driveway.

➡ Keep going past their car park on a lane, that runs between fields towards houses, to a junction in ¼ mile.

5 Follow the road ahead to rejoin the route at **8**

NATURE NOTES

The natural woodland lining the River Nevis contains native flora such as wild garlic – also called ramsons – that grows on damp banks.

Ragged robin is another wildflower that loves damp ground, but it needs to grow in full sunshine, not shaded by trees. Its pink petals are deeply incised, which makes the flowers look tattered.

Ringlet butterflies lay their eggs on wild grasses and can be seen flitting around damp meadows. Named for the eyespots on their wings, they fade from deep velvety brown to coffee-coloured as they bleach in the sun.

Hawthorn blooms in late May, its mass of white flowers also known as May blossom.

The rough grazing in Glen Nevis is ideally suited to Highland cattle, which are a hardy breed able to find nutrition in unimproved grassland.

Higher up, beyond the cultivated land and forest, the slopes of Ben Nevis and other hills are covered in heather. In summer, the most widespread species, ling, has mauve flowers that give the slopes a purple hue.

Ling (heather)

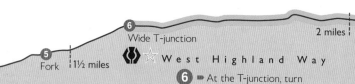

5 Fork ¦1½ miles

6 Wide T-junction

2 miles ¦

✡ ☆ W e s t   H i g h l a n d   W a y

5 ➧ Fork **right**, uphill, behind wooden forestry houses.
➧ Soon go through a gate into forest and follow a track, which bends right to a wide T-junction.

6 ➧ At the T-junction, turn **right** along a forest road, now following the West Highland Way.
➧ Where a track joins from the left, keep **ahead**, signed Braveheart car park, for ½ mile, to a fingerposted junction.

Highland cow

Wild garlic

Above: ragged robin
Below: ringlet

Four-way
fingerpost

Ben Nevis
Visitor Centre

2½ miles

Road

7 ➡ Turn **right** at the four-way fingerpost, signed Wishing Stone and West Highland Way.

➡ Zigzag downhill on a narrow, rough path beside a stream. Go through a gap in a stone wall and descend between fences to a road.

8 ➡ Turn **left** along the pavement for 200 yards, still on the West Highland Way.

➡ At a sign for Glen Nevis Visitor Centre, **cross** the road onto a wooded path back to the car park.

CATCH A BUS

KINLOCHLEVEN

This walk feels as if it is set even deeper into the Highlands than those near Ben Nevis. Although Kinlochleven is at sea level, high mountains tower on three sides. The route remains at a low level, following the banks of the River Leven to a splendid viewpoint looking down Loch Leven. Good paths underfoot mean you can concentrate on enjoying the scenery and heritage of the area, where drovers, soldiers and industrialists have all left their mark.

OS information	
🏃 NN 187617 Explorer 392	
Distance	2.6 miles/4.1 km
Time	1½ hours
Start/Finish	Kinlochleven
Parking PH50 4RU	Kinlochleven public car park, Foyers Road
Public toilets	Opposite Ice Factor, PH50 4SH (after ❻)
Cafés/pubs	Kinlochleven

Terrain
Tarmac and firm gravel paths around town; woodland and riverbank paths

Hilliness
Level throughout

Footwear
Year round

 Public transport
Bus service N44 from Fort William via Glencoe village, with bus stop on Leven Road, close to ① and ⑤, and on Wades Road at ⑧: shielbuses.co.uk

 Accessibility
Wheelchair and pushchair friendly throughout

Dogs
A good dog walk. No stiles

Did you know? The road along the south shore of Loch Leven, connecting the village to Glencoe, was only completed in 1922. It was started during World War I, with much of the construction done by German prisoners of war. They were housed in a camp about a mile up the River Leven from the village. Prisoners from another camp at Caolasnacon worked on the Glencoe end of the road.

Did you know? Historically, Kinlochleven consisted of two small villages – Kinlochmore and Kinlochbeg – either side of the River Leven. They were fairly isolated until cattle drovers developed a regular route through the mountains from Glen Nevis to Glen Coe. In the 18th century this was improved as a military road to move troops around the Highlands. Later, the route became the West Highland Way.

STORIES BEHIND THE WALK

☆ **Aluminium Story** The communities of Kinlochmore and Kinlochbeg were joined together as Kinlochleven when an aluminium smelter was built here in the 1920s. The smelter produced high-grade aluminium and in its early days employed 700 people, housed in the new village. By the end of the 20th century it was struggling to compete with larger, more modern smelters in the USA and was closed in the year 2000. Learn more in the Aluminium Story exhibition (thealuminiumstory.com).

☆ Aluminium Story

☆ **Hydroelectricity** Energy for processing aluminium was supplied by a hydroelectric power station, driven by water supplied from the Blackwater Reservoir. This was created by constructing a dam 1,000 yards long in the upper reaches of the River Leven. Water is fed from it by about 4 miles of concrete aqueduct and nearly 8 miles of steel pipe. When the smelter closed in 2000, the power station began to feed into the National Grid.

🅿 Kinlochleven public car park

Highland Getaway Inn ❶ River Leven ❷ ½ mile

➡ Go **right** out of the car park then turn **left** past the Aluminium Story building.
➡ At the main road junction, go **straight over**. Pass **right** of the Highland Getaway Inn to follow a lane **left** for 200 yards beside the river.

❶ ➡ Where the lane bends left past a red-brick building, bear **right** on a concrete path beside the river.
➡ Continue past a bowling green clubhouse and sports field to where the path surface becomes tarmac.

☆ **Ice Factor** Scotland's National Ice Climbing Centre, the Ice Factor, due to reopen in 2024, is based in the old smelter site. Climbers are trained on the interior walls coated with ice before tackling routes such as the North Face of Ben Nevis. Vertical Descents have created the first Via Ferrata experience in Scotland with fixed wires up the Grey Mare's Tail, while Kinlochleven Community Trust hire out electric bikes.

☆ **Water, water everywhere**
Kinlochleven is where the River Leven and many smaller streams tumble out of the mountains into Loch Leven. The most spectacular, the Grey Mare's Tail waterfall, cascades about 160 feet into a narrow wooded gorge. A sculpture near the end of this walk is of a Pelton Wheel, an impulse water turbine used to generate electricity. The spent water from the hydroelectric power station spills into the River Leven in a foaming tailrace (see also page 27).

View down Loch Leven
3 .... 4 5
Lane ¦ 1 mile   B863 viaduct

2 ➦ Keep **ahead** between wooden fences.
➦ At the next junction, turn **right** between railings, walking beside the loch to a bench and stunning viewpoint down Loch Leven.

3 ➦ Carry on to the next junction and keep **ahead** on the **left** side of a grassy triangle to reach a lane.

4 ➦ Turn **left** along the lane, through woodland.
➦ In ¼ mile, reach a metal vehicle gate below the B863 viaduct, built in 1929.

NATURE NOTES

The wet woodland by Loch Leven contains alder trees, which are happy to have water around their roots. The alder is the only broadleaved tree that bears its seeds in cones. Both cones and catkins can be seen on the same twigs.

Drier woodland, where oak is the main tree species, is the habitat of the pretty little yellow pimpernel. It has starry, five-petalled flowers and pale-green oval leaves.

The damp grassland and many streams around Kinlochleven provide good habitat for frogs. They move around by hopping, unlike toads, which walk.

Another lover of moist ground is the cuckoo flower, also known as lady's smock. The blossoms appear in April at the same time as cuckoos return from overwintering in Africa.

Eyebright is a much smaller flower, found in short grassland and along the edge of tracks. The white flowers have a yellow spot on the lower lip and purple lines, which guide insects to where pollen will brush onto them.

In high summer, soldier beetles are busy mating. They particularly like the flat flower heads of hogweed.

Hydroelectricty;
Kinlochleven
Power Station

Bri

Highland Getaway Inn

☆ Ice Factor

6

1½ miles

River Leven

Weak bridge

5 ▪ Pass **left** of a gate and follow the lane **left** then **right** to return along the outward route beside the river.
▪ Meet the main road by the Highland Getaway Inn.

6 ▪ Turn **left** and in 15 yards cross the B863. Turn **right** before the bridge to pass the toilets.
▪ Follow the lane beside the river, passing Kinlochleven Power Station. Cross a weak bridge and fork **left** to a vehicle bridge.

7 ▪ **Cross** the bridge and turn **left** by a wooden salmon carving, now following the West Highland Way.
▪ Keep **left** on a track that becomes Wades Road and runs past houses to a green and bus shelter.

Top: soldier beetles
Bottom: frog

Top: cuckoo flower
Middle: eyebright
Bottom: yellow pimpernel

er River
ven

Green

B863
bridge over
River Leven

Aluminium
Story

2 miles

West Highland Way

Pelton
Wheel

2½ mile

Kinlochleven
public car
park

8 ➥ Opposite the bus shelter, turn **left** on the West Highland Way, beside the river.
➥ Just before the road bridge, the path curves up to join a main road by an information shelter.

9 ➥ Turn **left** over the bridge then cross the road to a green with benches and a turbine wheel sculpture.
➥ **Cross** the green diagonally and return to the car park behind Aluminium Story.

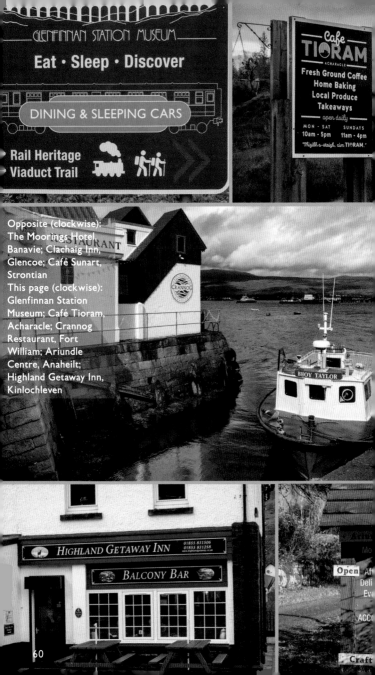

GLENFINNAN STATION MUSEUM

Eat · Sleep · Discover

DINING & SLEEPING CARS

Rail Heritage
Viaduct Trail

Café
TIORAM
ACHARACLE

Fresh Ground Coffee
Home Baking
Local Produce
Takeaways

open daily

MON - SAT	SUNDAYS
10am - 5pm	11am - 4pm

"Fàigibh a-staigh, aim TIORAM."

Opposite (clockwise):
The Moorings Hotel,
Banavie; Clachaig Inn,
Glencoe; Café Sunart,
Strontian
This page (clockwise):
Glenfinnan Station
Museum; Café Tioram,
Acharacle; Crannog
Restaurant, Fort
William; Ariundle
Centre, Anaheilt;
Highland Getaway Inn,
Kinlochleven

CRANNOG

BHOY TAYLOR

HIGHLAND GETAWAY INN   01855 831506
01855 831258

BALCONY BAR

Open

Deli
Ev

ACC

Craft

CLACHAIG INN, GLENCOE

Failte
Welcome

REAL PEOPLE

CLACHAIG INN, GLENCOE

← Reception

REAL HOSPITALITY

CLACHAIG INN, GLENCOE

Boots Bar →

REAL CRAIC

Café Sunart

Tea
Coffee   Bar   Food

WALL'S

WALK 8

GLENCOE

This walk combines loch and woodland trails. The red waymarked path round Glencoe Lochan is suitable for wheelchairs and pushchairs. A tranquil circuit, there are regular rest points where platforms provide an excellent view of the still water reflecting the surrounding trees and sky. The rougher, yellow-waymarked Woodland Trail climbs into the forest and passes a viewpoint looking east. Red squirrels, pine marten and roe deer live here and in spring bluebells carpet the ground.

OS information

🅐 NN 104593
Explorer 384

Distance
1.6 miles/2.6km

Time
1 hour

Start/Finish
Glencoe Lochan

Parking PH49 4HT
Glencoe Lochan car park

Public toilets
Nearest at the Glencoe village car park, The Carnoch, PH49 4HR

Cafés/pubs
Picnic tables. Nearest in Glencoe village, 1 mile from 🅐; The Clachaig Inn, and NTS Glencoe Visitor Centre café, both PH49 4HX, 2½ miles from 🅐

Terrain
Well-made path round lochan 🅐 to ❸; rougher, rockier path through forest ❸ to ❼

Hilliness
One steep climb after ❸

Did you know? The awe-inspiring landscape of Glen Coe is attractive to filmmakers. Its scenery has provided a backdrop for many blockbusters, including *The 39 Steps*, *Outlaw King*, *Braveheart*, *Rob Roy*, and the Harry Potter movies. *Skyfall*, where James Bond (Daniel Craig) returns to his childhood home, is also set in Glen Coe. While driving M (Judi Dench) there, he stops his Aston Martin DB5 and, in a memorable scene, they have a conversation gazing into the misty wilderness.

Local legend Ancient volcanic eruptions and, later, sculpting by glaciers have created dramatic scenery in Glen Coe, where river and road are squeezed between towering mountains. The glen's intense atmosphere makes it easy to believe in the old legend that the great Celtic hero Fingal lived here. He was the leader of the Feinn, powerful warriors of Gaelic mythology. His poet son, Ossian, found inspiration in the landscape and, like his father, is remembered in local place names.

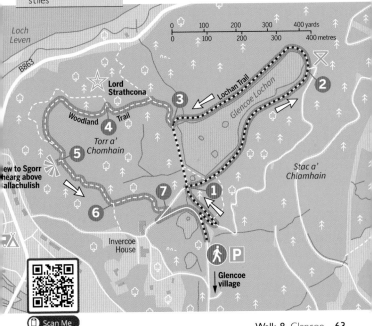

STORIES BEHIND
THE WALK

☆ **Lord Strathcona** The beautiful woodland of Glencoe Lochan was created in the 1890s by Donald Alexander Smith, 1st Baron Strathcona, for his wife Isabella. They moved from Canada to live here, but she was homesick for her ancestral lands. He planted conifers from the Pacific Northwest to make her feel at home but, alas, she didn't settle and returned to Canada.

☆ **The Glencoe Massacre** This tragic event involved the MacDonalds and Campbells, clans with opposite political views and a long history of feuding. After William of Orange became king in 1689 he required an oath of loyalty from Highland clans, many of which were Jacobites in favour of reinstating the Stuart monarchy. The MacDonald chief of Glencoe was late in swearing allegiance and this was used as an excuse to punish the clan. During the night of 13 February 1692, Campbell soldiers, who were loyal to the government, slaughtered 40 men, women and children, and burnt down the homes of those who fled.

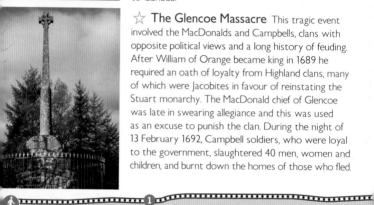

1 Track junction with a fenced stream

P Glencoe Lochan and Lochan Trail

Glencoe Lochan car park

➡ Take the path to the **left** of the map board, following red-ringed posts.

➡ In 50 yards turn **right**, gently uphill, and then sharp **left** in another 50 yards, continuing to a junction with a fenced stream (left).

1 ➡ Turn **right** for an anticlockwise circuit of the loch.

➡ Pass a picnic table then a viewing platform, and near the end of the loch, meet a minor junction.

☆ **Hamish MacInnes** The pioneering Scottish mountaineer Hamish MacInnes lived in Glen Coe and frequented the Clachaig Inn. Inside you can see the revolutionary ice axe he invented for ice climbing. He also designed a lightweight stretcher for mountain rescue (clachaig.com).

Ⅴ 🏛 Delve into the past

The MacDonald Monument was erected in Glencoe in 1883 to remember the clan members lost in the massacre. It is situated 200 yards along Upper Carnoch (PH49 4HU). Learn more about local history at Glencoe Folk Museum (glencoemuseum.com), in a thatched cottage in the village (PH49 4HS). The National Trust for Scotland Glencoe Visitor Centre (nts.org.uk), on the A82, also has extensive interpretation of history and landscape. Further east on the A82, a short but vigorous trail leads from a car park to Signal Rock (PH49 4HX), where the command for the massacre was given.

✕ Head of the loch

½ mile

🚩 Turn left to return to 🚶 ❸

❷ ➠ Curve **left**, past a picnic table, round the end of the loch.

➠ The path bends **left** again to run beside the shore, past two more viewing platforms to reach a junction at the next corner of the loch.

❸ ➠ 🚩 Turn **left** to reach ❶ and keep **ahead** for the car park.

➠ Otherwise, turn **right** by a memorial bench. Follow the main path (yellow-ringed posts) for 300 yards, uphill over rocks and roots, ignoring little side paths, to a junction at a sharp left bend.

NATURE NOTES

The wilder parts of Glen Coe are home to red deer, which like to shelter in the woods and around the village in winter. They are particularly visible around the upper part of the glen where it borders vast, open Rannoch Moor. Hinds and stags often congregate near the Kingshouse Hotel, where they can easily be photographed.

The North American conifers planted around Glencoe Lochan by Lord Strathcona included Western hemlock, red cedar and Douglas fir, which has a distinctive chunky bark with vertical orangey fissures.

The woods are rich in fungi, such as boletus mushrooms, which have pores on their underside rather than gills.

The native trees on the Woodland Trail (after ④) shelter bluebells in spring.

Bordering the path, where it's not too shady, you may spot delicate violets with their heart-shaped leaves.

More open areas with wildflowers are attractive to small tortoiseshell butterflies, which lay their eggs on stinging nettles.

Small tortoiseshell

Sharp left bend

☆ **Lord Strathcona**

④

¦ 1 mile

W o o d l a n d   T r a i l

④ ➡ Turn 90 degrees **left** with the main path, ignoring a lesser path (right).
➡ Continue for ¼ mile, crossing a dip and curving **left** with the main path, to a junction with a yellow-ringed post.

⑤ ➡ Detour to a viewpoint 25 yards **right**, looking towards Sgorr Dhearg above Ballachulish.
➡ Return to the trail, going **right** and continuing downhill for 300 yards to the next yellow-ringed post.

Top left: red deer
Top right: Douglas fir
Bottom left: boletus
Bottom right: violets

towards Sgorr Dhearg, above Ballachulish

Side path to hotel

Staggered track junction

6

7

W o o d l a n d T r a i l 1½ miles

Glencoe Lochan car park

6 ➡ Ignore a side path that goes right, downhill, to a hotel, and keep **left** on the main trail.
➡ Walk through tall conifers then descend to a staggered track junction in 200 yards.

7 ➡ At the junction, zigzag **right** then **left** across the track to follow the yellow-ringed posts on a path that curves **right** round a smaller, fenced lochan.
➡ Keep **right** to return to the car park.

WALK 9

ARIUNDLE, STRONTIAN

Strontian lies near the head of Loch Sunart and is the main settlement on Sunart, one of the five West Highland Peninsulas. This walk starts two miles north of the village and explores the woodlands of Ariundle Oakwood National Nature Reserve, whose name comes from the Gaelic 'Airigh Fhionndail' – the shieling of the white meadow. It is home to pine martens, red squirrels and golden-ringed dragonflies. Lovely views extend up the Strontian River to hills where lead used to be mined.

OS information

🧭 NM 826633
Explorer 391

Distance
2.9 miles/4.6km

Time
1¾ hours

Start/Finish
Ariundle, Strontian

Parking PH36 4HZ
Ariundle Oakwood National Nature Reserve car park

Public toilets
None

Cafés/pubs
Picnic tables. Nearest facilities: Ariundle Centre, Anaheilt, PH36 4JA (¼ mile from 🧭); Café Sunart, The Strontian Restaurant, and Woodfired Food Shack (1½ to 2 miles from 🧭 in Strontian, PH36 4HZ

Terrain
Forest track, boardwalk and riverside path (can be muddy)

Hilliness
Gentle descent to the Strontian River and a winding climb back up to the forest track

Footwear
Winter
Spring/Summer/
Autumn

Public transport
Very limited – bus
service 506 from
Fort William via
Corran Ferry to
Strontian (1½ miles
from ⬤): shielbuses.
co.uk

Accessibility
⬤⬤⬤⬤⬤⬤⬤⬤⬤⬤
Forest track
between ⑥ and the
car park is suitable
for wheelchairs and
pushchairs

Dogs
A good dog
walk. No stiles

Did you know? After the Free Church of
Scotland broke away from the established
church in Scotland in 1843, the local landlord
refused permission for its followers to build
a new church on his land. The solution they
devised was to have a floating church built
in Glasgow then towed to Loch Sunart. It
was moored offshore near Strontian and the
congregation were ferried out to it every
Sunday morning.

Local legend A standing stone outside the
Strontian Hotel has a large iron ring attached to
it. Reputedly this is the Punishment Stone (Clach
a' Phoanais in Gaelic), used particularly on market
days. If someone became troublesome, perhaps
from drinking too much, they were chained
here until they showed signs of repentance (or
sobered up!). It is also called the Branks Stone,
which suggests that the offender may have been
put in a 'branks' – a bridle-like device.

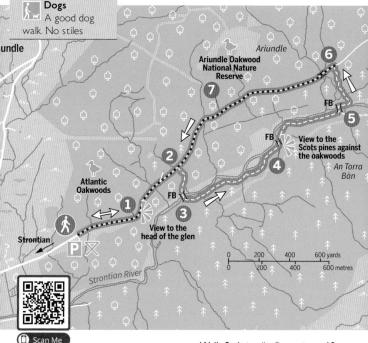

STORIES BEHIND THE WALK

☆ **Loch Sunart** Strontian lies near the head of 19-mile-long Loch Sunart, which gives its name to this central part of the West Highland Peninsulas. The entire loch was designated a Nature Conservation Marine Protected Area in 2014. Fishing is prohibited to protect endangered wildlife, such as the flapper skate, which can grow to over 6 feet across, and flame shell beds, whose shells open to filter water with red fern-like fronds.

🐦 **Atlantic oakwood:** Ancient oakwoods cover the hillsides along the north sho of Loch Sunart. They form one of the largest surviving remnants of the ancient oak forests that once spread alo the Atlantic coast from Spa to Norway. In this tempera rainforest habitat, tree trun and rocks are covered by mosses and lichens, kept mo by frequent showers. The natural habitat of Ariundle supports many rare species, such as the chequered skipp butterfly (nature.scot).

Main forest track — View to head of the glen — ½ mile — Footbridge (Strontian Ri

🚶 P ⊗ Ariundle Oakwood National Nature Reserve car park

Ariundle Oakwood NNR
🐦 **A t l a n t i c   o a k w o o d s**

➤ Walk to the information boards at the car park's far end and turn **right** along the forest track.

➤ As it bends left in ¼ mile, a superb view opens up to mountains at the head of the glen.

1 ➤ Bend **left** with the main track and ignore a side path, right.

➤ Continue past a post with an oak leaf symbol, which you follow throughout, for nearly ¼ mile to a path junction and marker post.

Corran Ferry

[St]rontian can be reached [fr]om the west (Mallaig [di]rection) or the east (Fort [W]illiam and Glencoe). In [th]e latter case it's a long [dr]ive by road around Loch [Li]nnhe. The quicker route [is] to use the Corran Ferry [a]cross the narrows from [O]nchree to Ardgour. This [fe]rry has existed for at least [?]00 years, when it formed [p]art of a 'drove route' for [ta]king cattle to market. It [pl]ies back and forth all day [a]nd doesn't need booking [(h]ighland.gov.uk/corranferry).

☆ **Strontian** The largest village in Sunart, Strontian's name comes from the Gaelic 'Sròn an t-Sìthein', which means Point of the Fairy Knoll. A path called Fairies' Road connects the village to Ariundle. About 200 years ago, a soft, silvery metal was discovered in lead mines here and named strontium after the village. It was used to extract sugar from sugar beet. Natural strontium is not radioactive, but its isotopes are, including highly dangerous Strontium 90, produced by nuclear fission.

SHOPS - CAFE
POTTERY
TOURIST INFO
TOILETS

View to the Scots pines against the oakwoods — Footbridge ❺

1 mile

❹

Ariundle Oakwood NNR

Path beside Strontian River

🐦 **Atlantic oakwoods**

❷ ➧ At the junction, turn **right** and walk down to the river.
➧ **Cross** the footbridge to a T-junction (where Fairies' Road leads to the right, into Strontian).

❸ ➧ At the T-junction turn **left**, between two boulders, still following oak leaf posts.
➧ Soon cross a small bridge over a side stream. Keep **ahead** on the delightful riverside path to another small bridge in 700 yards.

Walk 9 Ariundle, Strontian **71**

NATURE NOTES

This walk explores native woodland and open heathland beside the Strontian River. Both are habitats that have been heavily managed in the past – for forest products and agriculture – but now appear wild and untouched.

The heathland is full of wildflowers. The delicate-looking but hardy harebell grows on drier ground. Tormentil is widespread on Highland heaths, but being low-growing can't compete with tall vegetation. Wetter ground provides suitable conditions for marsh thistle, whose deep-purple flowers rise above the surrounding grasses and rushes.

The damp grassland and boggy heath support numerous dragonflies, such as the black darter, which can be seen flying on sunny summer days.

The woods are predominantly oak, but near the river mature Scots pine rise above the broadleaved trees. They are evergreen all year, and Britain's only native coniferous species. The seeds in their pine cones are food for red squirrels and crossbills.

Once you are under the woodland shade, it is striking how every rock and trunk is covered in moss, like a thick layer of green icing.

Atlantic oakwoods

T-junction with forest track **6**

Main forest track

2 miles **7**

1½ miles

Vehicle bridge with rushing stream; the oakwoods path leaves right, 10 yards after bridge, and rejoins the main forest track at **7**

Ariundle Oakwood NNR

4 ➤ **Cross** the footbridge with (in autumn) a view of evergreen Scots pine standing out against the oak woodland on the far side.
➤ The path (and the river) becomes rockier as it leads to a bench and bridge over the Strontian River.

5 ➤ **Cross** the bridge to a sign for Ariundle Oakwood National Nature Reserve.
➤ Follow boardwalk across a wet area with mature Scots pines, then wind up through oakwood to a T-junction.

Top: black darter
Bottom: tormentil

Top: moss
Bottom: harebell

Atlantic oakwoods

2½ miles

Ariundle Oakwood
National Nature
Reserve car park

Main forest track

Ariundle Oakwood NNR

6 ➡ At the T-junction, turn **left** along the track and soon cross a vehicle bridge (rushing stream).
➡ In 10 yards, an unmarked oakwood path leaves on the right: keep **ahead** for an easy walk; or go **right** for a more adventurous 700-yard route.

7 ➡ The oakwood path rejoins the main track: turn **right** if you've taken it; otherwise, keep **straight ahead** and follow the track back to the car park.

GARBH EILEAN

This not-to-be-missed walk is on the wild and remote Loch Sunart coast. If short of time, simply visit the wildlife hide for a taste of the rugged beauty and rich biodiversity of the area. With 45 minutes, you can stretch your legs by walking through the forest, which is gradually being restored from conifer plantation to native woodland. Two viewpoints with benches overlook the loch and there is a picnic site by the far car park at Ardery.

OS information

🧭 NM 742623
Explorer 390

Distance
1.2 miles/1.9 km

Time
¾ hour

Start/Finish
Garbh Eilean,
between Acharacle
and Strontian

Parking PH33 7AW
Garbh Eilean Wildlife
Hide car park, A861

Public toilets
None

Cafés/pubs
Picnic tables. Nearest
cafés in Acharacle
(6½ miles) and
Strontian (5½ miles)

Terrain
Surfaced forest
paths; boardwalk

Hilliness
Undulating
throughout, with
some short, steep
ascents and descents

Footwear
Year round

Did you know? St Columba is most associated with Iona, off the coast of Mull, where he founded a religious community in CE 563. But old writings suggest he spent time around Ardnamurchan, possibly before he reached Iona. A cave, an island and a well are named after him. One story tells that he landed to baptise a sick baby and blessed a nearby rock, which then bubbled up with water and never runs dry.

Local legend Two other forestry car parks lie between Garbh Eilean and Salen. One has a trail around Loch Na Dunaich, the 'Little Loch of Sadness'. This is said to be haunted by a kelpie (or water spirit), which usually takes the form of a beautiful horse. Kelpies are renowned for enticing children to mount them. They then become stuck fast as the kelpie plunges into the water to drown and eat them.

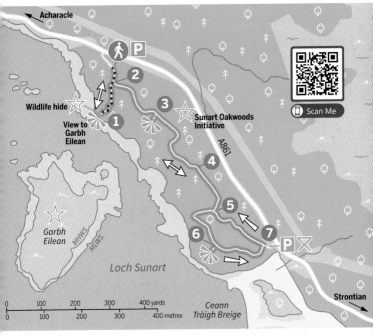

STORIES BEHIND
THE WALK

☆ **Garbh Eilean** Meaning Rough Island, this islet is one of many in Loch Sunart. Herons nest in its trees while seals and seabirds rest on the rocks exposed at low tide. Because it lies close to the shore, it is a good place to observe wildlife and a hide has been built overlooking it, accessed by an all-abilities path. Take binoculars for the best view and look along the shore below the hide for otters that regularly feed here.

☆ **Sunart Oakwoods Initiative** This partnership between public agencies and the local community aims to restore and expand the native woodlands around Loch Sunart. In the past, the woods were managed and nurtured by people for timber and charcoal-making, and bark was used for tanning. They survived because of the usefulness of oak trees, but became neglected when steel, oil and chemicals were used instead.

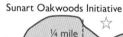

Sunart Oakwoods Initiative

Wildlife hide;
Garbh Eilean ☆
¼ mile

Garbh Eilean Wildlife Hide car park

P

Fingerposted junction

Bench and viewpoint

➤ Take to the smooth gravel path from the car park, past a map board.
➤ Almost immediately, keep **ahead** at a fingerpost to a boardwalk that zigzags down to the wildlife hide overlooking Garbh Eilean.

① ➤ Return from the hide, rising 150 yards to the fingerposted junction passed earlier.

West Highland
Peninsulas Collectively
known as the West Highland
peninsulas, the area is
often simply referred to as
Ardnamurchan, but Ardgour,
Moidart, Morvern and Sunart
are also distinct regions.
These peninsulas feel wild
and remote. Their rugged
mountains, heather moorland
and ancient woodlands are
separated by long finger-like
sea lochs and freshwater Loch
Shiel. The few roads linking
communities are winding and
mainly single-track.

☆ Ardnamurchan Lighthouse
Ardnamurchan Point is the most westerly
place in mainland Britain. A hazard to shipping,
its rocky shores are signalled by a 118-foot-
tall lighthouse. It was built of pink granite in
1848 to a design by Alan Stevenson, from
the famous family of lighthouse engineers.
The former keepers' cottages are operated
as a visitor centre, with a museum called the
Kingdom of Light (ardnamurchanlighthouse.
com).

Fingerposted
junction

4

5

½ mile

2 ➧ Turn **right** at the junction,
signed Ardery car park.
➧ In 175 yards, after the
path climbs and dips through
birch woodland and on
into oakwood, go **right** on
a side path to a bench and
viewpoint.

3 ➧ Take in the view of
mountains south of Loch
Sunart and a glimpse of
Garbh Eilean.
➧ Continue along the trail,
soon climbing over another
knoll, after which the path
flattens out through a stand
of larch.

NATURE NOTES

Oak trees have spreading branches, forming rounded canopies, and are long-lived. Their leaves have lobed margins and turn yellow then bronze in autumn. They reproduce by dropping hundreds of acorns. These germinate quickly and, if not eaten or shaded out by other trees, grow into a new generation of oaks. Acorns are a favourite food of red squirrels, jays and, traditionally, pigs, which used to be grazed in oakwoods.

Lichens grow on branches, trunks and rocks in the oakwoods of the humid Atlantic rainforest. They take many forms and are a sign of clean, unpolluted air.

In spring young shoots of male-fern unfurl, looking like the fiddlehead of a violin.

You will find blaeberry (the Scottish name for blueberry) growing in carpets on the woodland floor. It has deep-pink, bell-shaped flowers in spring. In summer these develop into juicy black berries.

Where conifers have been cleared, as is happening here as part of the native woodland restoration, foxgloves often grow more prolifically.

During the summer, look out in sunny glades for speckled wood butterflies.

Oak leaves in autumn

6 Bench and view to Garbh Eilean and mountains on the south side of Loch Sunart

¾ mile

7 Ardery car park

Fingerposted junction

5 ➡ Here, turn **right**, signed Ardery loop.
➡ The trail rounds a bend then rises up over a hillock with a side path junction on the top.

4 ➡ In another 100 yards, the path bends **right** to a fingerposted junction.